Working at the Supermarket

SO-DJF-965

This is Juan. He's from Mexico. Juan works in a supermarket after school. He's a cashier. Juan has to understand money and prices for his job. He's very good at math.

You do the math	**1.** Juan works from 4:00 PM to 6:00 PM five days a week (Monday, Tuesday, Wednesday, Thursday, and Friday). How many hours will Juan work this week?

It's 4:00 PM. First, Juan gets the carts. People leave carts outside the supermarket. Juan brings the carts back to the store.

You do the math	**2.** Juan earns $6.00 per hour. How much money will he earn this week? **3.** Juan wants to buy a DVD player. It costs $120. How many weeks will he need to work to earn $120?

Excuse me. Where's the yogurt?

It's 4:15. Juan helps his first customer. The woman can't find the yogurt.

"The yogurt is in the dairy section," he says. "It's on sale this week."

You do the math

4. Some yogurt is on sale. It is cheaper than all other yogurt. It costs $1.99 for six yogurt cups. How much do 24 yogurt cups cost?

Hi, Juan. How are you? Is the fish fresh or frozen today?

Juan sees his friend Ramon. Ramon shops at the supermarket two or three days a week.

You do the math

5. Fish costs $4.99 a pound. Ramon wants 2 pounds of fish. How much will the fish cost?

6. Ramon pays with a $20 bill. How much change will he get back?

At 5:00 PM, Juan hears a loud crash. Oh no! A customer tells Juan there is a mess in Aisle 10. There is juice all over the floor. There is broken glass, too. Juan has to clean up the mess. Juan does a good job cleaning up the mess. The floor is cleaner than before.

It's 5:30. Juan is using the cash register. He weighs the fruit and vegetables. The cash register tells Juan the prices. Customers sometimes pay with cash or checks. Usually, customers pay with their ATM cards or credit cards. It's easier and more convenient.

You do the math

7. Apples cost $1.59 a pound. How much do two pounds cost?

This ham is very good, Juan. Do you want a ham sandwich?

It is 6:00 PM. Juan will go home after he buys his dinner. Juan's mother and father work late. Juan usually buys something for dinner at the supermarket. Because he is an employee, he gets a 50% discount at the deli. For Juan, the sandwiches are cheaper at the deli than at a fast food restaurant. And they are more delicious!

Questions

A. Do you understand? Write your answers on a piece of paper.

1. What is Juan's job?
2. What does Juan bring back to the store?
3. How do customers usually pay for groceries?

B. Word Study. Find 4 comparative adjectives.

cheaper   _____   _____   _____

C. You Do the Math

Write answers to the math problems in the story.

D. Check Your Work

Compare your answers with your teacher's answers. Correct your mistakes.